Just An Imp's

Life Lessons From Spirit

Deb Keckley

DEDICATION:

To my husband for thirty seven years of loving me just the way you do.

Acknowledgment

For my many grandchildren. I hope your journey with whatever ability you may have will be as joyous as mine. Remember you are never alone.

When my way is darkest,
my soul takes me dancing
in the warm summer rain,
She reminds me what's most
important.
When my pain is unbearable,
my soul guides me to walk along
the ocean's edge in calm
reflection,
She shows my my strength.
When I am most afraid,
I shut my eyes and step beyond
my fear,
She reminds me that I am
forever.

By D.L. KECKLEY

CONTENTS:

1. The Last Eight Years

2. Jabber

3. Empaths, Suicide and Manic Bipolar
   Depression

4. The Wacky, Wonderful, Weird Way Of Spirit

5. Love You Too The Moon and Back

6. Do I Look Like The Devil To You??

7. She'll Be Back

8. The Case Of The Elusive Mask

9. Dogs Do Have Purpose

10. A Concept Of Heaven

11. ITC Today

12. Closing

****

You cannot always see your path from the valley unless you look to who can guide you from the mountain above.

Chapter One

The Last Eight Years

I have started this second book in my ***Just An Imp*** series about fifty times. It never seemed the right moment. Then I woke up one morning eight years later and here it is. It was like it had been all downloaded overnight in my mind. There was even a little sticky note that flashed. "Don't you think it's about time?"

I turned sixty in 2020. That's a number you got to wrap your head around. More than half a hundred. A moment where you wonder how it all went so fast because it still seems so fresh. It makes me laugh. I can see my mom so clearly now. How she must have felt at this age. Not sure I am liking it so much.

You know, I love the experience and wisdom sixty has given me. If I could have known all this at thirty. Geez, I would have saved a lot of falling on my face. Live and Learn. It is what we all do. I would imagine sixty won't stop that. It is the purpose of life to take "home" more then we came with. Raising ourselves to higher awareness.

My mind is as sharp as it has always been. I have a vivacious appetite for any learning I can get my hands on. Lately, it has been Royal British History. Don't know why. I just feel drawn. I love to spend countless hours building and decorating homes in my Sims 4 game. I find the architecture of Frank Lloyd Wright fascinating at the current moment. A few months ago it was Victorian architecture. I also discovered Polymer clay sculpting. Granted the first thing I made fell apart in the oven. It still came out looking like the Pegasus it was intended to be. A bit of glue, more clay, and a re-bake, he looks as if he were sitting drunk in a field of fermented apples. Yep, that's the story I'm sticking to.

I've changed a lot over the years. Taken steps that scared me to death. Yet, I have found myself so much more fulfilled for it. My eyes have opened to a bigger understanding that I create my life. That I am a part and whole of God. To quote Shakespeare's Hamlet, **"There are more things in heaven and earth, Horatio, Than are dreamt of in your philosophy."**

Since the moment of my NDE in 2007 I have known without a doubt. I am so much bigger than this life I find myself in at the moment. Seeing myself as an empty inanimate doll on a table, helped me to understand that I am only temporarily occupying this earthly creation we call flesh. I know I am a beloved creation, as are each and everyone of us. Thing is you must see that for yourself. You must see your own reflection in your creator. You have to stop feeling inadequate to be in is His presence and understand you are His presence in everything.

You have to see life as energy. Everything is energy. Only solid because we create it to be so. Our experiences feed the source, feed one another. Good, bad, or ugly. What happens is up to us. We could all at one time choose to see things in a peaceful light...and it would be so.

It takes every soul to quail the negative experiences we as humans have created in mass. To make a shift to a better reality. We could begin by taking small steps to move life toward something better. Starting with how we see one another. Not separate. Not race. Not Good or Bad. Just a part of the whole working towards the unity of the ONE.

You must apply to others the same as you want for yourself. One bad action creates another, and another..and so forth, and so on. Just as one good action creates rebounding good actions. Like a ripple effect. You see it all the time.

If in a moment of crisis, we can come together for a greater good, why can we not see this and recreate it in every waking moment?

I'm not here to tell you how to believe. See God as you have always seen Him. As a Man, as an Energy, as it suits you. Allow others their own beliefs. Just keep the faith. For faith is born in that special relationship you make with yourself and God (the source of all). Faith is finding the greatest you that you can give to others. The unconditional love and acceptance of your energy in every moment with everything. The not being perfect. But just being. You cannot better yourselves if what you believe in threatens and tears down the lives of others, for no good reason, except to show you are more powerful then they are. This is when you have no power. War in any form gathers nothing but grief, animosity, and destruction.

There's a pandemic currently. No matter what you think about its inconveniences or its conception in this crazy political climate that looms its ugly snoot and makes us tired, fearful, and just done with it all. Please, consider your family, your neighbors, a stranger who may not have the immune system to fight it off. A mask is a small thing to ask in those moments. I'm not fond of masks either. They are hot and sweaty and constricting. Still, I don't have the answers. Nor does anyone. So a mask it is.

These statements are my beliefs and thoughts. Each person must come to their own. In their own time. I can only state mine. Each of us will take what resonates with us and move forward with life. I hope with the grace to realize what truly matters for the greater good of all. So Listen, Love, and Learn.

****

What is you true Passion? You will never know till you follow it and find your true self.

Chapter Two

Jabber

I wrote my first book in 2011 and published in 2012. I had no intention of it being anything other then something my grandchildren could read in the future. My abilities are inherited...in the DNA. So just in case, I wanted them not to feel as alone as I have felt.

My father who was also medium passed in 1985. Yep, just before my ability to read spirit kicked in. So I had limited information to go on. Nor, did I ever contemplate it had been passed on to me. I knew what it was and that he did it. I understood energy and that I was just a soul having a human experience. However, with any ability one has, it needs to be learned, honed, and understood. Crap, I was still trying to figure out who I was as a married mom with two kids at the time. My life seldom centered mindfully on spiritual things. The only thing that caught me off guard from time to time was my pesky empathic ability.

Mediumship in my father's day was not as accepted as it is now. He did not have a practice. He just read from time to time, as nudged to do so. It wasn't a widely, fully discussed subject in our house. It was just a sort of understanding that it is what it is. We kept it in the family for the most part. My father's passing seemed to be my cue, that I was up. Ready or not.

I always wanted to be a writer. It was a passion of mine from the time I was old enough to write anything. I like to tell a story. So who knew my first book would be a true story. Got to laugh about that one.

I remember I asked a psychic once if I'd ever published a book. She said. "Yes, about your own life." That didn't seem what I wanted at all.

In retrospect, I probably did this all backward. I should have published after I went public with readings. Though I have been doing readings for thirty years now. Only about ten years of that have been openly advertised. The rest was practice, practice, practice. Though I got to say the universe has never failed to get me to someone who needs a reading. Seriously it is often so weird how it just happens.

In or around 2014 I opened for clients in my home. I became a sort of a Kitchen Medium. My favorite place to read a client is sitting at my dining room table. It feels homey and easy. So much like all the kitchen table conversations with my family when I was young. I think the spirits agree. I can do it over the phone. On the computer chat. Yep, even Zoom, as I have had to of late. Yet, no other place beats that table in my kitchen. I will be glad when I can get back to that. For a while, I fought Zoom even. Then I started feeling nudged and missing it. So I gave in. I have come to realize how much a part of me my reading spirit is. How good I feel helping others connect. You can't beat it.

It has been a battle at times to be devoted full time. Life has a way of interrupting you to take time outs for a good session of learning and not let you forget that despite any ability you have, you are still here to learn about yourself.

****

The Shortest path you seek is often the longest road.

Chapter Three

Empaths, Suicide, and Manic BIPOLAR DEPRESSION

My children have all grown up now. Two are married with children of their own. The last is happily in a steady relationship. I have been a grandma since I was thirty-five. We have five girls, aged from 22 to 4, and four boys from 21 to 4. Wow, hope I remembered them all. Pretty cool huh. Makes you look at each and wonder where they will all go in life. I hope with all my heart each is always blessed and happy. Though I know life will always have those teachable moments. It has to be that way.

I can't remember the exact date, but a couple of years after I published my first book my daughter Bambi was having depression issues. She suffers from Manic Bipolar Depression. A disease that rears its ugly head in such a way as to catch you off guard. The highs and lows are so swift and unexpected, that it leaves you shaking your head saying, "What the Hell was that about?!!"

It is a trying condition to watch from the outside. Even worse when you are the point of the anger in the mood swing. A simple comment you make can go from a molehill to a mountain in zero point sixty seconds. Not a place you ever want to be.

You want so desperately for it not to take over your child's life. I want her to have peace. It affects everyone around her, including herself so negatively. For all the information out there, I find there is no right answer. No exact set of rules to this disease. You don't always see a manic moment coming. Nor, did I realize this was the problem till her late teens.

Bambi's moody fits started when she was two. I just didn't understand it could be more than a temperamental, sensitive child. The information on bipolar depression in children wasn't out there. Nor did we have information that it is often inherited. I can look back now and know the line it came down.

An emphatic ability is reading emotional energy from our environment and others. We take it in, mull it around and learn from it. We do this without thought. The best way I can explain it simply is by these couple of examples. Have you ever been around someone that you were introduced to and all you want to do is walk away? Heed that feeling. Walk away from what feels off. It isn't for you. Have you ever been in a room full of people and you just wanted to run out the door? Or recognize someone simply by how they feel? There you go. Your ability to read any energy around you is a pretty powerful thing.

Most people come in with a dulled down version. Most of their lives it's only an occasional thing of knowing or feeling. Kind of like you often have with kids, spouses, and close friends.

It's like being on the same wavelength as them. Their day to day lives are fairly regular and uninterrupted.

Those of us who come in hypersensitive to all energy need to understand very early in their life we have tools within ourselves to control it. Not much help out there otherwise, except what you can glean from others who experience the same thing.

I told a doctor about this ability and how I know it affects my body. He looked at me like I was nuts. I did however have one doctor who listened to me about a hospital room I could not be in without being plummeted with dreams of soldiers who seemed lost, looking for family. It was like a line that never ended. Oddly, just across the street from the window in that hospital room is Old Fort Boise. Even my mother had stayed in that room once. She had complained about the constant chatter waking her up. They had to move her too. I didn't realize until much later that we had been in the same room until my sister was in the cancer ward across from that room.

It is so important to understand the energy that we are. The abilities we all have and the ways we can learn to control the energy, both around us and that we take in. These are some of the tools I use.

1. Learn to envision what you need your energy to do for you. Energy responds to guidance from our higher selves. I close my eyes and see my body fill with white light. When I reach the top of my head, I see a blue ball of energy rotating above it. This represents my higher self. I tell her exactly

what I need. I give her what is not mine to send back to the universe. Sometimes, I just see myself dusting off and handing it off in a bag. I recognize and say this is NOT MINE. You can also take a long hot shower. See it wash away any negative energy you are holding onto. Let it go down the drain. It feels awesome.

2: Except who you are. You have a purpose. Don't fight it. Take the energy in. Feel the emotions. Take what information you need and push the rest out of you. Ask yourself a lot. Is this a normal way I see and feel things? How do I feel today? Then when someone's stuff creeps in you'll know it isn't yours. Quickly deal with it, send it out, and be done. Don't dwell on it.

3. Take quiet time as often as you need it. Do what is your passion and just slip away from everything else. Meditation at it's best. I find it very healing.

4. Cry. Let go when it wells up. Crap I cry over everything. Go outside and scream as loud as you can, without causing the neighbors to call the cops that is. Let it all go!

5. Know your limits where energy is concerned. It isn't all good for you. There are vibrations of energy that off-center you and make you sick. You haven't learned how to raise and match it yet. There are energies on this planet that are like that too. You know it when you find it. Geo

magnetic. Often found in large deposits of rock. There is leftover energy of bad things, sadness, etc that have imprinted and play like a loop. Which is a lot of what people call haunted. There are lower energies that you don't invoke or play with for fun. Trust your gut. If it feels bad get away from it.

6. If you do see a spirit or can connect with them have rules. MY PLACE. MY SPACE. MY RULES.

7. Do quail the fear folks. Spirits are just like you. Just no longer in the body. Talk to them. Ask them what they need. You will often get a telepathic answer. I have on rare occasions heard them speak outside my ear without seeing them.

Knowing all this, my question about my daughter has always been, is she empathic and out of control? Or, is she hyper-manic with empathic tendencies adding to the problem? I believe it is the latter. Sadly, I can't prove it. For now, it remains simply what doctors diagnose.

The one thing that irks me, is I can be so aware of other peoples stuff. People I don't even know. Yet, I am so blind to my own families sometimes. I suppose this falls under the universal law of what you need to learn to help other people. Family life and dynamics is a good teacher. The lottery and psychic prediction clause are similar. To have something you want is to move forward knowing it is always yours at the right moment. What keeps it away is fears and doubts after you've asked for it.

As I was saying earlier. Bambi was having a bad bought of depression. I knew it. I could see it. She reassured me she was handling it by refilling her pills. She did refill them. After that she had a fight with a dear friend and took 90 of them, and went to bed. She had planned on permanent sleep. Even her friend returned to wake her. When she couldn't she just left her there. None the wiser I guess.

She told me later that it is very much like watching yourself go through the actions of suicide from outside yourself. You know its wrong, but it is someone else doing it. You are disconnected at that moment.

Her body shut down that day. Yet inside her, I think the struggle to survive kicked in. She had earlier called another friend to talk to him about the depression she was feeling over the fight. He had called back almost twenty-four hours later to check on her. At that point, she couldn't walk or talk or hardly move. Yet, somehow she had her phone close enough to her hand managing a finger swipe to answer the call. He immediately realized she was in trouble and called an ambulance for her. While everyone else in the home had gone on about their lives not even noticing she hadn't gotten up.

I didn't get the call till she'd been in the hospital almost full day afterward. I was dumbfounded, to say the least. This is not what I have taught my children. They know this is not a way out to solve any problem. I've had long discussions with them on suicide. Yet, I hadn't a clue this was about to happen.

I know how those parents from my readings feel. The guilt that creeps in. The only thing I could say to my daughter when I walked in that hospital room was, "What were you thinking? You know this doesn't solve any problem!"

Chewing her out wasn't the best choice I could have made. I was so angry at her. Yet, at the same moment so glad that she survived. Now she had a long road ahead of her. They put her in rehab on a seventy-two-hour hold.

Bambi's time in medical lockup made me see all this from another angle. One I hadn't even thought of it. It changed her. Instead of wallowing in her depression, she started talking to the other people, who were in her shoes. She was talking people out of bed and opening herself to listen to their stories. She was giving hope. Making friends. Being the empath I know she is.

She came out of this experience having learned that life is precious. That she is a bigger part of a whole picture. Even when sometimes the disease gets a hold of her. As it will do. She lends herself more often to help others in her situation. She understands the in and outs of this unpredictable disease. That helps her to help others. I'm proud of her and so very grateful to still have her in my life.

Suicide is often hardest on the family and friends left behind. There are often more questions than answers. It leaves us to wonder what could we have done to have prevented it. Please don't add blame on yourself. Please know they are alright on the otherside. Seek a qualified counselor to help you move through your grief. A medium is not the first answer ever. This comes in a moment and time when your energy is in the right space to hear the message. If you know anyone dealing with depression lend them your ear. Listen to what they are saying. Ask what you can do to help them down a better path of healing. Or simply suggest they call the number I have listed below. You can also visit the web site listed with this.

The National Suicide Prevention Lifeline.
1-800-273-8255

suicidepreventionlifeline.org

****

Spirit is who you will always be. Human is experiencing growth.

Chapter Four

The Wacky, Weird, Wonderful Ways of Spirit

Since I have been reading I've found that you should never doubt you got to me by a Spirits intervention. It's not coincidental. Always the message is just what you need right now.

Sometimes I get spirits who give information faster then I can keep up. Other times it's like pulling teeth to get them to give me information. If they were a shy person of few words, they probably will be in the reading. If they were big talkers, they are that way on the otherside. They retain their personalities and use them so that you can recognize them. It is funny what they will come thru with. I've often wondered if they got together and made a list of the odd and funny stuff their family member did while they were alive and since they passed. Yep, they watch you every day. Do they judge you? Nope. They cheer you on and send you love when the moments are tough and when they are happy. They know with bad stuff that, this too shall pass. So get used to it. You are likely the best family programming on heavens TV.

They're goal seems to be to make you smile and laugh. Get you to move forward with your life, by taking the first baby steps to see your grief and their passing just a bit differently. They are not dead, or far away, and they are always up for a good conversation. Talk to them. They will do everything they can to answer. It just isn't going to be words. It will be a myriad of little signs and symbols they send that remind you of them. You just have to softly allow it. Start with something simple. Something you associate with them. My mom is perfume, my sister a hummingbird.

I asked my brother-in-law the other night to answer a question I had by getting someone on TV to start talking about Spain. Sure enough, I was watching and Spain came up in someone's family heritage. He loved Spain. Be sure to say thanks, I love you when you get the message. There are times though they are just the kind that shows up in dreams, play with lights, turn stuff off and on, and move stuff around. It's their character to make stuff happen.

Animals will communicate by way of emotions and pictures or another family member. They really do understand much more then we give them credit for. I've had them so excited to be there that, they've rushed up and jumped all their energy at me. Feels just like you think it would. I also believe that they come back to us a lot more then we realize. I know my lab/husky mix Dolly is my Dalmatian Max. They have the same personality and behavior. Sometimes it's just the way she looks at me.

Not long ago my husband Randy was out in his back garage. On the ground, he found a dog tag. He was taken back by the name and address on it. It read Kimba. She was our white Shepard. Our first dog together thirty-some years ago. He brought it to me. That tag had long ago been put away in a small box in my room. This dog never lived at our current home. We've been here for over fifteen years. I was dumbfounded. It was not where I had lovingly put it in remembrance.

My husband said to me. "Kim's coming back into our lives as our next dog. It's a sign."

That coming out of him made me smile. He is probably right. Though I have had to restrain him from just going out for another dog. There's a perfect moment for everything. The thought of having any of my animals always in my life brings such joy.

Over the years my abilities have changed. I've seen spirit in my life, in many forms. Here lately it has been frequent. Perhaps because it doesn't frighten me. They were people. I will be like that one day. So why be scared. They are working hard to be seen. The least I can do is acknowledge them and ask if I can help. It's just the spur of the moment way they do it that gets me.

Randy's second-born son Scott came back into our lives after many years of not being able to see him. We were standing in the kitchen just chatting when I turned my eye to the hallway. A young man in an indigo work jacket walked down the hall as solid as could be. He didn't really turn and look at me, but I knew what he looked like. He impressed that on me. I heard in my mind car accident as he continued on his way across the dining room and right through the music room wall. I was so taken back that I asked my step-son if he knew anyone who had passed recently in a car accident. He explained he'd lost a friend in a truck accident almost a year prior. The description of him I gave, fit to a T. There we some messages for Scott that validated. Then in turn there was a brother who came down to talk to me soon after. I had drawn a picture of this spirit to give to him. He claimed it matched his brother in life. Not that I'm that great of an artist. When the brother went to leave I was urged to hand him a penny adding a say, "He wanted you to have this. He says it's not like the movie Ghost though."

It was later that evening in the quiet when everyone had gone to bed that the spirit of the young man returned to me. I was sitting at my computer and there was a loud metallic bang on the wood floor behind my chair. It sounded as if it had been slammed to the floor not dropped casually. It startled me. I turned to find a penny on the ground just behind my chair. I didn't have a change in my pocket, or at my desk. Yet, there it was a penny. I knew instantly I must of misinterpreted the message he intended to give his brother. I smiled as I said, "Okay, I get it. I guess it is like Ghost after all." Then I wrote an email to his brother retracting and correcting what I had said, as I explained what happened.

Last year I was waiting for the client to arrive for their appointment. I was just sitting, quietly meditating in a sims building experience. I heard a deep muffled voice down my hallway. I was the only one home. Nothing was on. Even the computer sound was off. I like to concentrate on my builds. I thought it odd, so I yelled out, "If you want to talk to me, You will have to speak clearly so I can understand,"

I really never thought more of it. About a minute later I hear the deep voice louder very clearly say, "LOW BATTERY."

The voice was so distinct. I got up to go see what on earth I had around the house that would say low battery. After a hallway, bathroom, and three-bedroom check finding nothing in my house that would speak or be on. I called my client. She had told me when she first booked that, she'd like to connect to her brother. I asked, "Was your brother's voice very low?"

She said yes it was. So asked. "Is there a reason he would use the term, Low Battery?"

She started to laugh. She told me this is what he would say when someone was very tired. She explained she'd worked an all-niter and was so tired that she was thinking about canceling her read. Apparently he didn't want that to happen. So he made me hear him so I would call her. That extra weird validation made sure she showed up.

A lot of my readings I don't remember. It is a not my stuff thing. There are however some that are so extra special they stick with me every day. Guess those are the ones that teach me a new thing or two. The next story deserves a chapter all it's own.

****

Love is never lost in death. It is connected to those who share it by a tether. Let it be your guide in life till you meet again in Heaven.

Chapter Five

LOVE YOU TO THE MOON AND BACK

Some stories in life unfold in such a way that envelopes you in it's meaning. Even when it is for someone else. You couldn't in a million years explain its synchronicity. But, I got to be a special part of one such amazing gift.

To love and be loved. It's what we all search for. We yearn for a person that will be our best friend. Our lover. Our world. Some of us find it easy. Others of us have a long search ahead till arrives. I have been lucky to know mine for the last thirty-eight years. I'd be lost without him. Not a day will pass that I didn't know how very loved I am. Regardless of how life unfolds for us along the way.

For some though how life unfolds with our partners passing, leaves us unsure and questioning, "Is that just the end? How do I move on?"

You have to understand all your loved one wants for you from the otherside, is for you to know how loved you always are and for your absolute happiness. Like I will say over and over again. You do not get to me by accident. It is carefully orchestrated by your loved ones because and I repeat, they love you unconditionally. It's all about you.

A young woman came to me for a reading. Her fiance came thru immediately. He explained how he had passed just shortly before their wedding date. Everything, he gave me validated. Yet, even then she wanted to hear one thing. She asked, "What did he use to say to me all the time?"

I explained to her that, it isn't long sentences they give me. It is more pictures and feelings I must interpret into what they are trying to get across. Then I asked him to show me. He showed me the moon. Just a moon. When I told her that, tears began to flow, and she validated to me he always used to tell her, I Love You To The Moon and Back. Above everything, it was all she needed to hear.

Many months later my husband who was working with junk cars at the time was cleaning one out to take to scrap. He found a little silver box all wrapped with a purple bow under the seat. Looking inside he thought it was something I might like so, he brought it home to me.

He gave me the box with an explanation of where it came from, I opened it. It was a silver necklace with a half-moon hanging from it. Now, I'm not a big jewelry person, nor did it feel like it belonged to me for some reason. I looked at it. Thought it was nice. Then, put the lid back on, setting it aside.

The next morning I opened the box to inspect the necklace a little more. I got closer to it and realized it had writing all around the edge of it. Reading it I kinda laughed. I sort of recalled that saying coming through a reading once. I put the lid back on and set it aside again. Not more then ten minutes later my phone rang. It was the lady to whom I'd given that particular reading too. She was having a hard day. She explained It was the anniversary of what would have been their wedding. We talked awhile and she hung up feeling a bit better. A few minutes later my eye was drawn to the box again. I got this overwhelming feeling of being pushed. I'm sure his spirit was yelling, "Wake up! I need you to do something for me!"

I suddenly realized why that little box ended up with me on the anniversary of this couple. It was a very special gift for her. He wanted to say, "Yes, I truly, LOVE YOU TO THE MOON AND BACK!"

I instantly picked up the phone calling her back. I explained how this little box had come to me. I didn't tell her what was in it though. I only explained I felt an overwhelming nudge by her fiance that, I had to give this to her today on her anniversary. It was very important. She gave me her address and I almost speed to her apartment.

I handed her the little box. She opened it and read the inscription on it. We were both balling hysterically at this point. She said to me with big alligator tears in her eyes, "He had promised just before he passed that, he would get me a necklace to match this bracelet."

She held up her arm to show me a little bracelet that matched that necklace perfectly. She hadn't worn it at the reading. So I didn't know she had anything like it. There were a lot more tears from both of us that day. We had a long conversation, with a few more validations he threw in for good measure. Turns out even the little box it came in had meaning. The purple bow and silver box were the wedding colors she had picked.

On the drive home I was reflecting on all that had happened. How he had perfectly made everything happen in sequence. How lucky I was to get to be the one to deliver this little gift that, held so much meaning between these two. To be able to feel the strength of this love they have for each other. Time might have been cut short for the two of them. But, for the rest of her life, every time she sees the moon. Her heart will swell thinking of someone who loved her, and who taught her the meaning of it unconditionally from the otherside of the veil. He helped her to move forward in life to find her next chapter. The next love of her life. You can be sure he will be cheering her on till the day she comes home.

****

If you are afraid what I believe will change you unwillingly.
Don't worry, that will only happen if you choose to believe with
me.

Chapter Six

Do I look like the Devil to you??

My husband, Randy and I have had many friends in our life together. Many, many of our friends have passed as the years fly so quickly by. Too many in my view. Cancer, why does it seem like cancer is always the cause? There is something seriously wrong about that. I can't even tell you why it seems so wrong the amount of cancer you see. I've had it twice. I was lucky it was all caught early. My husband also had prostate cancer. He beat that too. Please, catch it early, it's so very important to the outcome.

Neely lost his battle in 2013, due to cancer, brought on by Agent Orange exposure in the Vietnam war. I don't want to go into harping about it. This is not what this story is about. I just know there we several awful things throughout the years that he experienced with this exposure. He also had PTSD. It caused insomnia. He would get caught in very real dreams reliving a lot of his experiences. He never talked about it much. It was obvious his time in that war was traumatic on him.

Neely Vaughan was one of the sweetest, calmest people I have ever meant. Patient beyond measure. Unless you pushed him. He was after all also a Taurus. He was a mentor to many kids in his life. It says so on his stone. Some people are just father figures naturally. I've lost track of all the kids he has taken in over the years. Randy also, ended up inducted into teaching trucking. Working on cars. Music, etc. Neely's three boys, his nephew Gary, and Robert, who was one of the boys who grew up around both men, are working or have worked with us in our business over the years. The other funny thing that we didn't realize as time has changed it. The lot we rent for our business is the lot Neely lived on. Funny how life works. I think he's still looking out after all of us in one way or another. Wouldn't surprise me a bit.

Neely and Randy played together in many bands over the years. Like Randy. Neely's voice was very individual and powerful. I think he knew every old country song ever written.

Fun times those days. His wife at the time, Roxie, and I became close friends also. The four of us spent many hours together. We had babies at the same time and just shared life as friends do.

Roxie and I have sat at the bar watching our men playing and singing a lot, over the years. I can recall a moment on stage once that the much shorter Neely stood up on a chair, took off Randy's cowboy hat, and kissed him on top of the head, during a break between songs. One-off the wall comment or another would get the two started clowning around for the audience.

One night there was a bar fight at the end of a gig. Some drunk guy commented about the music with, "You think you're something huh?"

Randy made some comment that half ignored the guy. It pissed the guy off. He stood up to face off with Randy, his fist drawn back. Somehow, I was behind the drunk guy and got shoved back and stepped on by a boot when my husband got off the barstool to take the drunk on. I don't think he realized just how big and tall my husband was too him till that moment. By that time Neely had seen what was happening and came behind the guy just as his punch went flying. He grabbed hold of the drunk's one finger putting him on the ground in pain, begging. Fight over. I would think he learned the move either in the military or overseas during the war.

Neely's good friend Larry Hagadorn and his wife Brenda joined the band. Let me tell you, Hag, as we called him for short, could play a mean guitar. Brenda played bass always beside him. Hag also taught Randy to play bass. The group of four close friends became six for a few years.

We usually ended up at Hags for Jam sessions. Brenda always made tacos. It was her thing to feed everyone in her house, all the time with tacos. When I think of Brenda, I always think of tacos. She loved to cook. I was at her oldest daughter's house one Christmas season a couple of years ago. Seems she has taken the love of cooking and her looks from Mom.

We have just recently reconnected with Hag and Brenda's kids again. You can bet that wasn't an accident. The kids lost there mom and dad young. It's nice to know we can be around for them and help remind them of good times with their parents. It helps us all quail the sadness of change, their physical loss has left behind. It helps to bring a little of that music back into all our lives.

As time went on. Neely and Roxie moved to Michigan for a while. Then came back. They divorced. But, remained friends for all the rest of his life. This was good for their boys. Neely even was there to greet Roxie's daughter when she was born. For Neely, that little girl was as much a part of his life as any of them. When he had the boys on visits, He had her too. He just had such a big, loving heart.

Roxie eventually remarried and moved a couple of hours away. Neely reconnected in his later years with a woman he'd known a long time. They eventually married and settled down out of town. Where he became very involved in her church with her.

Their religion was very strict about what was deemed right and wrong behavior in life. Which, I admit. Not my cup of tea. Nothing wrong with it. I believe each should come to God and their beliefs in their own way.

It is a bit off-putting to understand a belief system makes you unacceptable unless you vow to be someone you are not. That's the way I felt when I was around them. Made me very sad. Because, I have always, always looked up to Neely as a friend. I learned a lot from him.

When I was in the hospital for about a month. His wife came to visit me. She is a nice lady. I'm sure she meant well that day. However, there must have been something off-putting about her to the nurse that day because no one had ever asked me if I wanted visitors before. They just let people wander in. Even ones that came once. Yet, the nurse asked me that day if I wanted a visitor. She felt so troubled about it to me that, I turned the visit down. I found out later that it was Neely's wife. Perhaps my Guide knew this was not the right energy for me in that moment, and just intervened. I was putting all my own energy into healing. Maybe, I didn't need any more then what I was doing for myself. I do thank her for all the prayers. I know she and Neely sent many. Prayers are always helpful energy. Just sometimes, we need to be deep within our own faith to heal and not have that momentum interrupted. It was a just me and God thing in that room for a month.

Neely was no longer allowed to play in bars due it not fitting with his church teachings. This and just the general uncomfortable feeling like our friendship with Neely was no longer in his best interest, I think it is what led to the rift in Neely and Randy's relationship. On one hand. Neely needed to follow the beliefs he had devoted to in the church. On the other. Randy needed to have his musical partner and long time friend in his life. Hag and Brenda were no longer here. I suppose Randy felt left in the cold. He struggled inside with that. So it just ended in a fight that never made any sense.

A couple of years later we got wind that Neely was suffering from cancer. I asked Randy if maybe he could see his way around to reconnecting with his old friend. It's important to not be holding anger for someone you care a lot about. Especially when that anger is misdirected by its reason. I urged him to make some very good last memories with his friend.

We did reconnect. Had him over for several Jam sessions with his kids. Enjoyed the moments. Made good memories. I even got to sing with them. I don't think Neely ever realized I could sing.

Neely, Randy, and I decided to go camping together up at Arrow Rock Damn. The reservoir that year was let down so low that, it was a half-mile of dry, sandy riverbed before you could launch your boat. So we ended up parking our campers and setting up camp in the middle of the riverbed to keep an eye on the boat in the water.

Neely's energy level didn't let him do too much, for too long. He did get out and fish with us a few times. The rest of the time he spent on his own in camp resting in his camper or out visiting around the campfire with us. It was a nice time to catch up and just talk about life. Play a little music and kickback.

One of the first nights at dinner. I gave Neely my book to read. I felt it might help him with thoughts he wasn't talking about with us. I've been in that place, where he was. You have many thoughts run across your mind. Including ones about what lies beyond. There is distinct knowledge in the back of our minds that, knows life just doesn't stop. We are so intricate as human beings that, it's hard to fathom we cease to exist at death. Truly, when you get my age life seems to pass by in a blink. It seems rather unfair to believe you only get one life. I've worked hard to make me the best me I can be. Even those that do believe when you die you cease to exist, have moments of bouncing that around their minds for truth. No one could convince me they don't.

I have always found my book ends up where it will do the most good. It was all I asked of its energy when I published it. Just be a seed of thought in the right moment. However, I had a moment of doubt this time. Yet, a very strong nudge I had to follow.

I talked with Neely about my experiences as a medium. I explained to him my own beliefs about life and death. Even about my very personal relationship with God, and how his energy works in my life. I just thought, screw it, what can it hurt for him to know. It didn't seem to matter that I knew his own deep beliefs didn't support mine. Because I also knew the real Neely Vaughan. The one who had seen the spirit of his father many times. The man who was a listener, and a mentor. Perhaps he needed a bit of mentoring for the end of his life. A little extra *Food for Thought.*

When I had laid it all out for him. He slyly smiled and took the book. He was so calm as he very simply said, "You know this is the Devil's work?"

It must have been the look on his face. He didn't say it with real seriousness. It wasn't in a condemning or judgmental tone. I kind of laughed and replied playfully, "Neely Vaughan, as long as you have known me, do I look like the Devil to you?"

He just quietly laughed at me. I finished the conversation as he took the book and started toward his camper, "All I want to ever know from you, is that you are at peace."

Our last camping trip was cut short the next day. A freak wind funnel dropped into the canyon. It stirred up the dust and sand in a whirlwind in a split second. I couldn't even see my little Sheltie, to pick him up and make it a few feet back to the camper. When we finally got to the safety of the camper, it was rocking and shaking, as the wind and sand battered it. I wondered if there would be anything left when it was over. It was one wild half-hour ride. A little damage was done, and a mess that had to be clean up. After that we packed up and headed home.

I'm pretty sure Neely read the book a bit. I saw it next to his bed, as we were packing up. It had that distinct bent back to read look a paperback gets. I didn't know it would be the last time I'd see him.

The day of Neely's funeral, the family gathered for what I suppose they thought would be a small simple gathering of friends. It was outside in the Veterans area of Dry Creek Cemetery. It was not small in attendance. He was well-loved by most everyone his life touched. I never think of him without a smile. I'm glad he blessed my life. I'm sure others feel the same way.

I was sitting there listening to the eulogy. My eyes were drawn to Neely's wife. She was seated two rows in front of me on the same end. Standing beside her was a transparent bodily shape of light. It was Neely's height and shape. He stood there I suppose listening, as everyone spoke. His energy was touching her ever so slightly. He was lending his love and support to her. I hope she felt that. I hope they all felt his strong presence in their lives that day and still do.

A few months later I was talking to one of his kids on the internet. A video link popped up. The title drew my attention.

Amazing Grace. A song I've heard Neely sing many times. One the son I was just talking sang for him at his funeral. So I turned it on realizing this was not a version of Amazing Grace I was familiar with. It had new words mixed with old and a new chorus. The music was much the same. However, if ever a spirit could orchestrate music to tell a story about their journey home. It was Neely.

The lyrics to this song are on the next two pages. Please look it up on Youtube and listen. It will move you in it's beauty and message.

Amazing Grace (My Chains Are Gone)

Chris Tomlin
Amazing grace
How sweet the sound
That saved a wretch like me
I once was lost, but now I'm found
Was blind, but now I see

'Twas grace that taught my heart to fear
And grace my fears relieved
How precious did that grace appear
The hour I first believed

My chains are gone
I've been set free
My God, my Savior has ransomed me
And like a flood His mercy rains
Unending love, Amazing grace

The Lord has promised good to me
His word my hope secures
He will my shield and portion me
As long as life endures

My chains are gone
I've been set free
My God, my Savior has ransomed me

And like a flood His mercy rains
Unending love, Amazing grace

My chains are gone
I've been set free

My God, my Savior has ransomed me
And like a flood His mercy rains
Unending love, Amazing grace

The earth shall soon dissolve like snow
The sun forbear to shine
But God, Who called me here below
Will be forever mine

Will be forever mine
You are forever mine

I could not have been given words that meant more to me. It was if Neely was speaking through song directly to me. He was telling me that, indeed he was at peace. He taught me that it isn't how you believe. Only that you believe. This was Neely's parting gift to me.

****

Sometimes you open your mouth and your Higher self speaks a better truth.

Chapter Seven
She'll Be Back.

The three youngest grandchildren are, Phia, who is five. Noah, who is four, Rainy, who is also four. I look at my grandchildren and see little individual souls. I know each has graced my life with purpose. It makes no difference how I got to be their grandmas. I just am the one they call grandma. So I have the responsibility of teaching them many little life lessons.

I'm a bit over-protective, a bit strict about what they get into. The guy who cut our trees said I was something to the effect of a drill Sargent. That was a bit harsh. I was trying to keep them seated in one spot so they could watch the tree fall, and not jump up and run to it as it did. None of them can sit still for more than two minutes. Nothing unusual in that.

My way of parenting, I always thought was a little less structured than my mom's. She raised her kids thru the fifty's and sixties. She was nearly forty when she had my brother and me. We were expected to have manners. Be respectful to our elders. To not tear up the house. Roughhouse outside, not on the furniture, and help with chores. My kids had many of the same rules. Most importantly, the one thing I wanted to be sure I was to my kids was one of my mom's best qualities. You could talk to her about anything. Although with my mom I think we taught her more in certain areas then she knew was a thing. She was our rock. Our sounding board all our lives. She did not give advice and say follow it or else. She gave advice and said, "This is my experience. Maybe you could try it this way first."

Don't get me wrong. My father was an authoritarian ruler in my house. Typical King of his castle. Etc, etc, etc. However, let the King overstep his rule unfairly, and the Queen took the scepter in hand. "All Hail the Queen!"

Driving a Taurus to their breaking point is never a good thing. It wasn't with Mom and it isn't with me, her equally Taurus daughter. We have unpredictably, explosive tempers. We are sweet, and patient people most of the time. All we ask is, don't cross the line that hurts people we love. Please don't force me into being or doing things I don't agree with. Do not think you have any rule over me what so ever. That would be so foolish to even consider. I know the last time I came unglued everyone on the porch got up and ran in the house. I heard my son-in-law, Jason say as he departed for safety, "Oh Damn! Grandma means business!"

I want you to understand I have messed up with my kids more then I can count. It has been a live and learn road as it is for all of us. I wouldn't expect my children to not have the same road ahead with their children.

I have observed that the dynamics of parenting are so much more challenging than they ever were for me. What used to seem such an easy answer, is not so much anymore. Kids come in more advanced in a way I can't put a finger on. Society is also so much different. I can't keep up. I have gotten stuck in my old ways. It's like pulling a tooth to change the way I might see things in this new age.

Rainy as my son and daughter-in-law call miss Lorraine, came into their lives after their boys hit teenagers. She was adopted into the family as a baby, from within the family. Probably, all I can explain about that. Family takes care of its own. My daughter-in-law is so good with kids that, she has taken in and cared for just about every kid in her family over the years. She is the one every-one trusts with their kids. She has magic. Aunt Stacy is the one you want, believe me.

Rain is spunky and sassy. Independent and tough too. She may be four but, I swear she has the debating skills of a twenty-year-old. She will wear you out in less than ten minutes. I'm not sure who adopted who first, but Rainy calls my son and daughter-in-law mom and dad. It's the one steady thing that she has always known.

I had told Jesse and Stacy long ago there was still a little girl to come. I didn't say how. I thought I'd missed on that prediction. She took a long time to get here. I'm glad she made it. She's going to wear them completely out before she grows up. I can see it now.

My daughter Bambi has wanted children for a long time. Her first marriage had three little boys from her husbands first marriage. She took the job on like a champ. She helped work through the welfare system to get them out of foster care and back to there dad. These poor boys were messed up emotionally. I don't know all of went on between their mom and dad relationship, but it was apparent it was damaging to them.

My daughter was determined to help these boys overcome the obstacles and regain a normal life. These boys were setting little fires and hoarding food in their rooms. Stealing and purposely breaking things. A lot of behavior you'd expect from traumatized kids. There was learning issues and withdrawn behaviors to work through.

Little by little, over time you began to see vast improvements. Personalities started to shine. They were doing great in school. They loved Bambi and Bambi loved the boys. To her, she was now mom. It didn't seem their mother even cared. You never saw her come to see them.

Like I've said you can be particularly sightless with your own. I didn't see the warning signs until much later. What you might think was the fault of just one parent who swears it was the other's fault. Turns out to be a complete lie. Seems Daddy had anger issues.

One night my husband and I got a phone call from the police. There had been a physical altercation between my daughter and her husband. You know when the cops are calling it is never good.

When we arrived we found my daughter being checked by paramedics. She'd been strangled so hard that her eyes were bloodshot and her neck was bruised. I know married people fight. I also know my daughter can fight hard and loud. But this was inexcusable in my book. This is my child. I told her that her and the boys were coming home with us. I also told her she had better look for a divorce lawyer. I know men like that don't stop. She told me what was worst of all is at least one the boys saw the choking happen.

Over the days she backtracked a lot about filing for divorce. I was happy at least he was in jail. He also had a warrant out in another county, so he was going to be in jail awhile.

Bambi's biggest thing was the fear of losing the kids or them having to go back to foster care. She had no legal right to keep them. They were just in her care while he was in jail. After much hard thought. She did file for divorce and held her breath that maybe, just maybe the system would give her guardianship. They were good kids. They were thriving in her care. Seemed that should amount for something, if no other family stepped up to the plate.

She had them I think nearly four months in her care. Then one day out of the blue the mother called telling Bambi pack them up I'm coming. She had the paperwork returning custody to her. There was nothing Bambi could do. The boys did not take this news well. They didn't want to go back their mother. On the day she came, there were a lot of tears. The little one hid and they had to find him. There were a lot of little boy's faces plastered to the back window waving and crying as they pulled away. I honestly think it was the start of the deep depression that had led to Bambi's suicide attempt. It was a blow to her heart she did not know how to handle.

I've never known Bambi to do anything that she didn't invest all of her into. She loves deep and hard. Fights a cause till she has no choice but, to give it up. Even then I don't think she ever really gives it all up. Despite that bipolar thing that gets in her way sometimes, there is a shining, beautiful soul. She would fight the battle with you to the bitter end if you needed it. She understands the inner struggle people find themselves in far too often because she's no stranger to battling her own. I know my daughter firmly planted seeds of love and care for those boys. Maybe they will bloom bright as time passes.

As life goes on we find our strength to move forward. With enough love and support, most of us can beat our demons down. Get them behind us. Bambi did just that. She met her current husband, Jason. It wasn't long before she got pregnant. She was so excited.

Bambi and I felt it was a little girl's energy around us. One that was very excited to come to us. Sometimes you just know. There is a circle of energy we are connected to with our family here and on the otherside. Sometimes we get wind of the whispers. I don't think it's an uncommon occurrence among families. I remember when I was pregnant with Bambi. My mom decided, out of the blue to sew a little girl's blanket. She told me that she knew it was a girl. You do not question a mother's wisdom. It is what it is. She wasn't wrong. Even I have dreams or feelings telling me when a new family is coming in. Sometimes, even the gender.

When I got pregnant the last time, I knew it was a boy, based on a very vivid dream I'd had two years earlier. My grandfather told me. He also told me what I should name him and why.

My mom had a very special bond with Bambi. I know her spirit is often with her. When she left this world it was Bambi her spirit soared through, like a big hug when she left. It filled Bambi with so much emotion she doubled over very aware of what had just happened and uttered in her tears, "She went through me!"

It was Mom's way of saying, "I know you need me and I am always here."

It didn't surprise me then to be sure she was holding that baby in her arms on the otherside. Even helping to prepare that soul for her life ahead. Spirits have often come through in readings saying they were first to hold a child before they were born. Similarly, Spirit also will come through about a child who has past with little to no life experience and validate that energy is within the family circle.

Bambi and Jason went in for a checkup, so Daddy could hear the baby's heartbeat for the first time. I was anxiously waiting to hear about it. I remember the way they came through my door that day. The energy entered the room before they did. Her first words through her sobs were, "Mom, she died! There's no heartbeat!"

I opened my mouth to give comfort and the only thing that came out was, "She'll be back."

I was kinda flabbergasted. That wasn't was I was going to say. I was about to give comfort. Not resound she would be back. Like some ultimate prediction. Yet, there was a reassuring feeling in those words I recognized was true.

Miscarriage is very common with first babies. It's nature's way of knowing when something is not right to carry a baby to term. It was hard to grasp why they would let us know this energy, then strip it away. I don't think I will ever know why. I only know what I felt to be true.

I went with them to the ultrasound to confirm. There was no little heartbeat. No movement. Just a silent little temple, where once and energy had come in to give it life.

I wondered why my daughter had to go through this lesson. Mentally they should know that she is not equipped well, to handle such deep loss. That questioned deepened as she took the medicine to help her abort. It wasn't enough. Only enough to give her horrid cramps. They had to give her more. It took her two long agonizing days to finally abort. I was peeved at the otherside. I needed an explanation from my family. From someone higher up. So I said. "Hello God?"

The answer that came back was again a calm peace, "She'll be back."

I suppose it isn't for me to know the lessons each is to pull from their experiences. I am to know only my own. In those lessons, we are to find our strengths. Our faith. How much more will you love if you know there are no guarantees of how long someone will be in your life?

A child you must give all of who you are too. They are energy so close in vibration to yours that, we often forget that they are individual beings. We'd like to think they will be little reflections of us. Make us immortal in some way to show the world, *I was here*. In truth, they are reflections of the love you feed them. So you better feed them well. Hopefully in that way they reflect only the best of what we give them in advice, lessons, and experience. Before long they bloom into their own. It's a tricky balance to be the disciplinarian, teacher, and friend you so want to be to them. If you pull it off without a hitch...Kudos to you my friend. You are rare indeed.

Three months later just after Bambi and Jason married, they became pregnant again. Baby girl did indeed come back. The same wonderful little energy I knew before. Stronger than before. Strong enough to like a couple of my other grandchildren, suggest the name she wanted to be know by.

Sophia Cecelia Rose made her grand entrance into this world five years ago via c-section. I remember nervously sitting with my husband just outside the operating suites. There is this moment when the first cry is heard and you know that little being is a part of you. So familiar. Like no other babies cry. Definitely a big voice like her grandpa. She has her daddy's great big smile and looks like her mom. Where am I in this mix you ask? In her heart where I will always and forever live for her.

Bambi went on to help bring Jason's then five-year-old daughter from his first relationship more solidly into their lives. As I said, she is always a catalyst for the right thing getting done.

Lilly is sweet, a little shy, and quiet. She loves to hang out and help the adults. I got to say she is one of the first grand kids to offer to do dishes and want to help with cooking no questions asked. Her grandpa has taken a shine to her and she to him.

Thirteen months after Phia's birth Bambi and Jason had their son Noah. A mop-headed blonde, who hates a haircut and is a bit of a wild energy. He practically fears nothing. Just yesterday his sister got stung by a wasp in the playhouse, No sympathy there. He was more interested in being right there to help grandpa get rid of the wasp nest.

Noah was born in the sign of Aries. Lately, he's decided he doesn't like to hug anyone in authority without provocation to do so. Grandpa hatched a plan to get his hugs, by bribing him with the one thing he always wants at our house. He said, "Noah, if you want a Popsicle from me, you have to hug grandpa now and then when he asks."

Of course, Noah agreed. Why not. This worked well for a bit until one day grandpa asked for a hug and Noah refused. Of course, grandpa reminded him of their agreement.

Noah looked his grandpa square in the eye and replied, "The popsicles are all gone."

My daughter and I laughed so hard. That backfired. You only take a hug from Noah when he's in the rare mood to give one. He's an Aries. He's going to out-think you on every level. This Grandma butts head with him on the listening thing. He is so independent, we are afraid he will drive off with the car when we're not looking. LOOK OUT WORLD!

As life unfolds before us, know in your soul, no matter what, there is a reason for what happens. There are right moments in time for all things. You may not always know for certain a lost soul has returned to you. Yet, from time to time it does happen. Sometimes, you only have them for a very short time. You may not understand why bad things happen but know that there is always peace for them. A short entrance is often a lesson to ready you for a bigger challenge. To get ready for blessings you will know how to handle better when they arrive. Celebrate each fully. Truthfully, you are never given more then you can handle. You are given what will teach you and move you forward towards goals you set for yourself before this life began.

****

Someone you love is always going to show up to let you know it is all going to be okay. where they come from might be another story though.

Chapter Eight

The Case of the Elusive Mask

My sister Rose married very young to a man named Ed, in 1957. They remained married until her passing in 2011. I was barely a toddler the first time I meant Ed. He was this bigger than life energy, with an Alabama accent that swept you in for a good old down south hug. You just never questioned with Ed that you were loved and excepted by this big brother. His life had been one of taking care always of younger brothers and sisters. So he was well versed in that art.

Most of my life growing up Ed was in the air force. So, Rose and family, we shipped around all over the country. In fact, my niece Cindy was born in Spain. There were times when during a move they came to stay a few weeks with us. Eventually, when he retired they moved back to Idaho to be close to family. At that time I was 18 and very pregnant with my first son Jesse.

Ed was always someone to look up to. He readily loved to teach things. To talk your ear off. If I was in a spot I could count on Ed to help me figure it out. He was another one of those people who were natural mentors to everyone around them. He was always solidly my brother. It is how I always thought of him. Looking back on his presence and my sister's presence throughout my life. I realize now more than ever how under-appreciative I may have been about needing them In my life. How much they meant to me. It took their passing to write the words I felt for them at their respective eulogies. The things I wish I had made clearer when they were here.

When my sister passed he was lost and brokenhearted. He tried to remain upbeat and continue on for his family. It got better with time. Yet, there was always that sad undertone in his energy.

About three years after my sister passed he developed lymphoma. I can honestly say I didn't see that coming for him ever. He did well with the chemo. Though it was rough on him. He was in his early seventies. It's hard on anyone. Harder the older you get. He made it through. He graduated in remission. They threw him a celebration.

I don't know what went wrong, but very shortly after that, he got sick with some respiratory thing. I'm pretty sure it had everything to do with a lowered immune system. It could have just been a simple cold germ that got out of hand. He was admitted to the hospital and eventually put on a ventilator.

The night before I went to see him in the hospital I was laying in bed. As clearly as I have ever heard a voice in my mind, I heard him say. "I DO NOT WANT THIS!"
I replied out loud, "I hear you, Ed. I will tell them."
That was probably a bigger task I promised then I could accomplish within the family. I mean I get it. I do. I see both sides of things.

Everyone needs hope. Time for family members that are farther away to get there to see their loved one. But also, I can walk in his shoes. To be on those machines. In a position where you cannot make your own choices. Afraid of forever being just a vegetable in a bed. That was not for him. He needed to have his choice. He made it very apparent by pulling his ventilator tube that night I heard him in mind. His kids were perfectly aware he did not want it.

They had put him on a c-pap when I went in to see him. Because he refused to allow them to put him back on the ventilator. He was even trying to take off the c-pap mask. He looked so unlike himself. So sick. Trying hard to make his point and unable to speak. All I could say was,
"I heard what you said to me last night."

He looked at me for a moment and gestured for me to take the mask off. Something I couldn't do for him. I leaned in and took his hand and whispered what was my last words to him, "Thank you for being in my life. I love you more than you know."

I couldn't rally myself to return for the last gathering of family around him. He got his wish when all goodbyes had been said. He had them remove the mask, understanding perfectly well he would not survive it. He was ready to be with my sister on some island in Spain somewhere. A place where their life together first started. One of the last places they went together before Rose got sick. A promise I suppose they might have made to one another to meet in the next life.

About three years ago my husband was recovering from back surgery. The doctor had stopped a regular medication on him that he has taken for a way to many years just to abruptly stop it. It threw him into a withdrawal that altered his state of mind. I realized he needed help I couldn't give him. At the same time, it frightened me to the point I wasn't sure how to get him the help he needed without him thinking I was betraying him in some way. It gave me a fright I have never experienced in my life. Luckily, he did get to the ER and got admitted for help and he was back to normal after a day. What a relief.

Maybe it was the fear. Maybe I was just too tired and it lent to activate what probably already was wrong, to begin with. That night I got one nasty headache at the back of my skull I batted it all night with relief. I got up that next morning. Went to the bathroom. My head started to feel like millions of little electric shocks were going off. I passed out face down in the tub.

How in the world I managed to wake up again and make it to my phone in the living room I do not know. I just knew I had to, as I was all alone and in trouble. I managed to call 911. Managed to remember at least my son's work number and stay awake trying to breathe till the ambulance arrived. I was supposed to pick up my husband from the hospital that morning. So I had to make sure someone got him for me.

At first I think the paramedics thought it was just an anxiety attack. After all, they had just picked up my husband and taken him to the hospital. I was alert. Although, Iseemed to have no strength. My arms were like noodles that just wanted to flop around.

When they loaded me into the ambulance. I was in this calm place I seem to always end up in moments of severe illness that bring me close to death. It really is a sweet place to be. Maybe my calmness threw the paramedic off. He seemed surprised I had a mind on me to instruct him to pull a credit card from my purse and hand to my step-son with instructions to get his father from the hospital.

They ran a quick EEG and called it into the doctor. The doctor radioed back. Step it up. Bypass the ER and go straight to the cardio Lab. It was lights and sirens after that.

I was perfectly aware. I saw my daughter, as I came down the hallway towards the lab. I tried to mouth it's all okay to her. I saw the paramedic standing at the door watching very concerned. Clothes started coming off. Leads on. I heard the nurse say. She's in complete heart block. They went to work. Amazing how fast they can get that stint in.

Crisis adverted I was wheeled to Cardiac ICU much to the relief of my family. My poor husband. I think I nearly gave him a heart attack. My sister Kathy, my kids we all gathered around the bed. I felt bad I know how bad this scared them. I spent two days there and then was sent to a regular room in the cardiac ward.

When I first got to my new room. I realized quickly I had an alarm on my bed that sent a nurse flying in if I tried to get out. Bummer. I was actually hoping I could get up and run around finally. I was feeling perfectly fine.

I was probably in my room less than an hour when a bald man in a hospital gown wandered in. At least I think he did. Seems like he was suddenly there.

He was an older man. I couldn't really see his face. He seemed to keep his head away or down from my view. I offered a nice, "Hello,"

He started to kind of dance around and get a bit closer. He held his hand in front of his mouth as he got closer. He said, "I was looking for my mask. I have misplaced it."

I thought maybe he had been in the room prior to me. Perhaps they moved him. I replied, "No I haven't seen a mask."

He twirled a little and stepped in, head down close to my bed. I still could not make out the features of his face or the tone of his voice. He felt so sweet, so calm natured, so oddly familiar. He simply replied, "It's okay. It is kind of a Halloween thing anyway."

I chuckled and with that, he twirled a bit away from me. He seemed to be heading back to the door. I heard the curtain move, but I can't say I saw him actually leave that way. I was a little dumbfounded. I had to think about it a bit. I told the nurse when she came by. She just looked at me with a smile and said, " Oh really." Like she thought okay it must be the drugs. I really wasn't on any drugs that would have caused that.

The thought crossed my mind later that if he had been a cardiac patient wouldn't the alarm have gone off and the nurses have been hunting him down?

I pondered on this incident many a day after I came home. There was just something about it that was off. Something way too familiar about him. What was it? Then it dawned on to me. The one and the only person I knew who made it his job to get into someone's hospital room where he wasn't supposed to be. Who had casually strolled into the labor room when I was trying to push my first baby out like owned the place. The guy who fought the mask on his face every step of the way and who's oldest daughter Cindy had passed at the age of 32 the night before Halloween.

My God, it was Ed. Funny wonderful Ed, making his presence known. Letting me know he was okay and that he had been reunited with his daughter. I already knew Rose had been there waiting for his arrival. This would be so him.

Like I wrote earlier I asked him to tell me it was really him by getting someone on TV when I turned to a random program to talk about Spain. Then I would know that yes it was him. It took all of five minutes for him to get that to happen. What more could I want to convince me indeed it was him?

So we are at the end of the story. *The Case of the Elusive Mask* is solved. Love you ED!

****

Faithful friend I am grateful you touched my life if only for a very brief moment in time.

Chapter Nine
Dogs Do Have Purpose

If you have never seen the movies **A Dog's Purpose** and **A Dog's Journey** starring **Dennis Quaid,** you are missing not only a good tear-jerking story. You'd also be missing something I have long talked about. Dogs do have a purpose. I'm sure it is not just dogs. I would imagine it is any beloved pet in our lives. I also bet that more often than not that pet picked you out, rather then you picking him them. I'm sure you think you did. But did you really? Think back? How many of your pets came into your life in an odd and usual set of circumstances. You can bet it was arranged from a soul level.

Here are forty years of my experiences with my furry friends. When you are done with this chapter spend some time and remember all you have learned from them that bettered your life. They are the best teachers of unconditional love.

I have always had an ability to energetically connect with animals. It isn't a big thing. Just that animals trust me. Understandable because animals always connect on an energy level first. They can read you like a book.

Dogs are my favorite buddies. Don't get me wrong I love all kinds of animals. But, dogs for me are the best

Communicators. Although I haven't ruled out getting to know a Dolphin or two in my life.

When we decided to get a dog in our first year of marriage. Randy thought a White Shepard would be nice. They are beautiful animals. His reasoning was that he'd meant one once who chased him up a fence and bit him on the butt. I say it was a memorable meeting.   That dog's name was Kimba and so we named our dog Kimba (Kim for short). Not the way I would have decided on a pet. But in Randy's way he was trying to move past the fear of dogs that the butt bite encounter had left.

Our Kim was a sweet, lovable, Nanny for my kids, and a strong protector to me when my husband was gone trucking. I didn't train her to be that way. I figure it must have been her purpose in our lives. She picked us. It wasn't the other way around.

The day I went to find our dog I stepped into a yard full of multicolored Shepard pups. They were far to busy wrestling each other to even notice me. I did kind of think that was odd. Pups are generally all over anybody who looks like they might play with them. There were so many pups I wondered where to begin. So I just sat down on the ground to see what would happen? Still none of them broke from playtime out of curiosity just to come to see who I was. So I waited. It only took a few minutes and from out of the puppies this little snowball came running toward me and climbed straight into my lap. I needed no other sign to tell me that this was the pup who wanted to be in our family. I've never regretted that decision once. But I wish the time we get with them wasn't so short.

When I lost Kim I asked her in spirit to send us a dog just for our family. What I got was a clumsy, dopey Dalmatian named Max. Full of energy and so loving he'd lick a thief and hand
everything you own to them neatly tied up in a pillowcase. I knew Kim sent him because the first night I said go to bed and he got up and headed right for the very corner were Kim always slept. I didn't even have to explain to him where that bedroom was.

Max's real purpose was to be my constant companion during my two bouts with cancer. One that cost me a kidney. The other a complete hysterectomy and then three weeks later was followed by a bleed out from an irritated duodenal ulcer. That was that month in the hospital I was talking about.

Max rarely left my room when I came home. I'd often wake to a cold nose nudging me maybe to take deeper breaths. I had a lot of pain medicine and nausea medicine in me. So I suspect my breathing wasn't normal to him. You couldn't have asked for a better nurse then Max.

Each animal was with me twelve years or so. Each one was so painful to lose. You often wonder why you should do it again. But the quiet they leave behind is deafening. So again I asked Kim, "Send me a friend."

I discussed getting another animal with Randy. He suggested Shelties or Shetland Sheepdogs were cute. He'd had a dog growing up that was a part collie and so Shelties always reminded him of his family dog. The thing is Shelties rarely end up in pounds. They have their own rescue centers. We had none in our state at the time. Just high dollar, very well papered pups available from breeders. I was still working at the time. I felt it wouldn't be fair to get a pup and not have time to potty train consistently as I had done with Kim. I just had to trust that if it were to be. One would come into our lives.

Two weeks in I brought up a Craigslist add pretty much by accident. It opened to the picture of a little 14-month-old male Sheltie who looked like Lassie. The add said they were looking to re-home him. They had too many pets and the owner was having a baby. He was fixed, potty and crate trained, and obedience trained. All of what I needed. They weren't asking much and were less than 20 miles away. So I grabbed Randy and headed to their house.

When we first arrived this little twelve lb guy, bowed to Randy in that let's play stance and that was all she wrote. My husband fell in love. That pup was coming home with us. His name was Hoku. Hawaiian for Star. He had delicate features with dark olive-shaped eyes that spoke volumes.

Hoku was very much his own dog. He was one of those animals that if he had been a human. He would have been a highly intelligent, easy going British professor. Complete with a monocle. You see Hoku had one eye he always squinted when he looked at you. He never much liked his head patted, but he'd turn and offer you his butt for a good scratch instead.

This dog never wanted to be in your face. He just wanted you to be with you. Lay at the side. Listen to you talk to him or gladly submit to a long brushing. You could do anything to that dog. He'd just lay there. Vet's loved it. Never a whine or a complaint from him.

Shelties have a lot of funny little quirks. They spin before they pee. I always figured they had to get all that hair going in one direction so they didn't get it wet or dirty. They sing If you talk to them often and in just the right way. They will reply in a very high howl pitched like a song. They will change the tone as they talk to you or give a low, choppy howl almost under their breath in discontent. They also take on or mirror their owner's personality over time. So what I got as the years passed was a dog who matched me energetically. We were in rhythm with one another.

Hoku's purpose didn't seem as clear to me. Maybe he was just around to teach the simple act of getting older and just enjoying what you have accomplished and had. To just love.

Four years ago Randy decided he'd like to adopt another dog, a Husky. So off to the pound we went one day. One of the very first kennels we looked in had this very sad dog glued into the far corner of the kennel. Her face with its big sad brown eyes was Labrador. Her ears were pointed and half droopy. One was cocked higher than the other. Her coloring was the black and light tan like a Siberian Husky. The tail was curled and laid on her back when she stood up.

She looked so pathetic and afraid. We talked to her a minute to try and get her to come close. She wouldn't. We continued looking down the line of kennels. I happen to glance back. Those big brown eyes were peeking out around the corner watching us. We'd go back and she'd go back to the corner. We move away and she'd watch us intently. We were so drawn to her. Finally, We decided we should get her out of the kennel for a walk and see what happened.

They told us her name was Dolly and all they knew about her was she been picked up running loose. Nobody ever came looking for her. So she was up for adoption.

Dolly perked up once she was out of the kennel. Randy lead her over to a bench and started to talk to her. She laid her head in his lap and she was ours.

I'm not sure Hoku was as thrilled about meeting his new sister. He just looked at us like fine, whatever. All Dolly wanted to do was sniff and play. We figured they'd warm up to each other. They did. Hoku did his thing and Dolly did hers. Hoku was a little old man at this point in his life and he played the part. All he cared about was being close to me.

Two years ago my little old man got very sick. He dropped half his weight and couldn't get enough to drink. The vet diagnosed diabetes. With fluids and insulin, he seemed to get better. I had to learn to give three shots a day in the scruff of his neck. He was so good about that. Never winced. I know his little neck had to be sore.

Three weeks in with the insulin shots and just before Christmas he seemed to not eat much and he slept pretty much all the time. My heart just couldn't go through deciding on having to put him down. I had to do it twice before. I prayed to not have to do it again. I told myself over and over he would be fine. He just needs time to get adjusted to the insulin.

Christmas day came and went. We got up the next morning to go outside. Hoku walked out on the porch and just lost his bladder. Something he never did. I put out food. He didn't seem to want it. He just wanted to sit.

He was panting a bit so I thought maybe his feet hurt him. He was having problems with hard growths on his feet. We had to keep them trimmed down or they were painful. I checked them. They seemed fine. I decided maybe a nice brush massage would help. He seemed to like it and relaxed. I gave him his shot and we continued the day.

Maybe and an hour later I looked in the living room at him to see how he was doing. I found him distress. He was panting as if his life depended on it.

My heart skipped a beat. I knew he was in trouble. I scooped him up and headed to the vets. I called my husband as I pulled out to let him know. There was heavy construction on the road I had to go down to get to my vet. I stopped at the first stoplight. I felt Hoku paw at my arm from the back seat. I turned to look at him. He wasn't breathing hard anymore. It looked as if he had a big smile across his face. I asked, "What baby?"

Hoku drew very close to me locking his eyes to mine. He never broke his gaze with me. He just seem to melt slowly onto the floor. The light went green. I put my hand back on him. He felt different. Too soft. My heart dropped. I remember I cried out, "NO! NO! NO!"

I looked for anywhere to get out of the construction in the bumper to bumper traffic. I couldn't get out where there wasn't barriers or equipment. I called my husband upset. I was trying not to let the tears out so hard that I couldn't see where I was going. I just had to let him know. He'd want to know too. All I could do was continue to fight the heavy traffic and construction to get to the vet as fast as I could. It took me over five more minutes to go the last mile.

I sped into the parking lot finally and stopped the car. I jumped out and pulled Hoku up upon the seat. I could see he was gone. I just dropped my head down into his fur and balled.

My husband had been out in the tow truck at the time. He probably was not too far behind me at the time I last called. He came racing into the parking lot beside me. His reaction was much the same as mine. Just to hold him and cry.

I suppose someone in the vet's office looked out the window and saw all the commotion. My niece who was a vet tech there at the time came out and took Hoku back to try and resuscitate him. I tried to tell her it had been way more then five minutes. She came back to the room to ask how much we wanted to do to try and bring him back. I knew It had simply been too long if he wasn't responding. Randy and I conceded to let him go in peace.

We were allowed to go home and bring Dolly back with us to see Hoku's body. I thought it might help her understand why Hoku was suddenly gone from our lives. They did get to be buddies. They ate together all the time. I was afraid Dolly would stop eating if he wasn't there. Dogs do grieve.

There was something about losing Hoku that has made my grief harder to deal with. It was the way he made the extra effort to say goodbye. To connect with me eye to eye. Soul to soul in those last moments. The smile he had on his face stays with me. I love all my animals. But this one stole my heart completely.

I'm pretty sure he knew how much I was hurting. The next day as I was unloading a bag of dog food in the garage. I glanced down at my feet to see Hoku just standing there. Tail raised and wagging. Looking so well and happy. It was only just a few seconds. But It helped ease my heart to know he was Okay. That was the very first time I'd seen one of my animals in spirit. He was one of a kind that one.

Our Dolly is still with us. I swear she is Max returned. There are just so many similarities that remind me of him. Like Max she just wants to be loved all the time. She is excellence with the grand kids and like Max she'd lick a thief and hand them everything we owned tied up in a pillowcase.

She seems to me to be the type who needs a playmate. She's acted a little lonely without Hoku. I have a feeling there will be a buddy for her one day very soon. Maybe, just maybe Kim is coming home for one more adventure with us. One more purpose.

****

From seemingly nothing, is everything.

Chapter 10

A Concept of Heaven

Do me a favor and just humor me in this chapter and imagine if you will, that everything is energy. Nothing can or will exist separate from the other. What was and is, is only now.

Energy is multidimensional and any given outcome in creation has many recreations of itself. Each just a little different from the other. As our energy learns or our perception of occurrences changes. We can shift our realities to one that includes our new truth. Therefore, everything we know as solid and real is simply a creation from within our own being.

Think of life as a very lucid dream. Perhaps that is why when we have Near Death Experiences everything seems so much more real. So much more vibrant in color. We instantly recognize it as our truth. Our home.

The concept is. What if you have never really left heaven? What if your experience now was a slumber in which you choose to experience life separate from your true home? Creating a kind of virtual reality in which you separate partially from your higher self and load that energy into the template of the life you choose to lead at that moment. Think of the earth as your chosen base game. Though it is only one of many worlds that are either separate or that can be a part of that base game.

Think of it as the source, (God) having universally created from all that is for others of his creations to come together and learn from.

Perhaps because we are offshoots of the source himself, with the same creative energy we found a desire to experience what life would be on our own. Maybe we are all just impetuous teenagers trying to grow up. So the source allowed us to seek what we need to learn as separate beings. Thus we can go home and understand Dad was really not so wrong.

I know this analogy is way left field to our current beliefs. To think of being whole with anything but ourselves is near to impossible. Individuality is how we see ourselves. That's why we have names and strive to have our own unique personalities that announce we are different than anybody else.

Who really knows the answer? I would imagine there is a good reason we don't. We aren't ready for any truth beyond what we currently understand to be our reality. In my experience, not even Spirits offer a clear view. Just a glimpse now and then. Yet there are if you choose to believe other entities that can and do communicate to us from other worlds, other dimensions.

Think of it this way. We are all spirit. All from the same source. If you think you are God's only creation. This much I know for certain. You would be wrong. I will leave it at that.

Everyone always asks what and where is Heaven? That I presented you with this particular concept is a way to make you think about the infinite ways Heaven could be for someone. It remains within your belief system and therefore you create how it will be for you. I know from experience it is a place of peace that cannot be described adequately and compared to this life on earth. I know those that have gone before me are still able to communicate with me. That I am loved beyond measure. Anything more we just have to know that from seemingly nothing is everything.

****

One Day Heaven will have cell service.

Chapter 11

ITC Today

Instrumental Trans-communication is sort of an umbrella term in the paranormal research community that covers a wide variety of voice communication from spirit. EVP (Electronic Voice Phenomena) has been the most common way. You turn on a recording device and ask your questions. You wait a moment in silence and play it back. Spirit uses the energy around them to speak and it translates onto the recording. Where you didn't hear a voice while recording you will get one when you listen back. Sometimes it is very clear and understandable. Sometimes not.

It was Frank Sumpton who took spirit communication to a new level with radio sweeps in 2002. His Spirit box, which used radio channels in a fast rate sweep allowed the spirit to pick random words and string them into communication in real-time. It was one of the clearest of its kind in that era. Unfortunately, he passed far too soon to really move to further levels with his work.

The Franks Box today is rare, expensive, and coveted. His work has led the way to internet apps that sweep internet radio in much the same way. There are some that are quite clear. There also other apps that scan through a bank of random words or a bank of random language sounds that help the spirit to communicate.

Now I don't want you to think you are going to just pick one of these apps or boxes up and automatically be able to communicate clearly. One. You have to know what you are listening for. Record each session and run back through it, often to hear what can't be deciphered or even heard in real-time. Most of all you need an energy relationship with spirit. You have to learn to raise your vibration up to meet theirs. They will pretty much always meet you half way. That means you are opening up your energy with them, just as any medium does. You need a sort of rapport with them. It's not all about the box itself.

With spirit boxes it is hard to tell exactly what dimension you are reaching or whom you are really communicating with. You want to be energetically protected with light and prayer. Stating your clear intention for whom you are trying to reach and what is allowed around you or through the box. Just as I never start any of my sessions without a long talk with God, my guides, my family, and even Jesus about being with me, and allowing only the greatest good through. I also invoke angels as protection to not allow anything that serves a negative purpose to come through. If you are not in a good place you will attract the same negative to you. I never read when am in the wrong headspace. I know at the very least I can become very ill for a time from something negative. What else I have never experienced. So I couldn't tell you. I do not make it a point in my life to dwell on it. I dwell only on the greatest positive that I can achieve with it.

One of the biggest contributors to the field of ITC is a gentleman by the name of Steve Huff. You can find him on YouTube on Huff Paranormal. I have watched him over the last ten years slowly developing his spirit boxes. To date his inventions are some of the clearest communication with the spirit you will find.

Spirit has shown him over the years how to create just what they need to communicate through these devices. The little by little they have advanced on that.

There was a time that Steve didn't really believe in mediums. I really get a laugh about that. Because today he is as much a medium as I am. Though he says he's not. He still is shown things within his mind's eye before the spirit will validate them on the box. He has grown to where he will actually see the spirit, describe them then the spirit will validate on the box. He communicates with loved ones for others on a monthly Patreon session. He gets a lot of validation back on his comment section from those who watch. Really they come through no differently on the box then they do for me within my own reading without a box. The difference being it's cool to hear in real-time.

With time Huff has gotten better and better at it. That's how it works we get better as we go. I hope you will check out this amazing guy. Watch him from his beginnings to now. He has about 800 videos on YouTube documenting all that he has learned and how his invention of his Portal all the way to his Astral doorway boxes came to be.

One day because of his work I am very sure we will just turn on a device and be able to talk to our loved ones on the otherside. Wouldn't that be amazing?

****

Open your heart to listen and only take what you need.

Chapter 12
Closing

Well, that has been the last eight years of my life. If you want to learn about my early life and the road I have traveled along the way. Check out book one I mention in the first chapter, on Amazon. I'm sure that a few years more done the road there will be more. In the meantime, I will continue to work to help others connect with their loved ones. Helping them to move forward with their lives, toward their own new and amazing experiences.

We are spirit. When you leave this world you will not have a body that defines you as a human being. You will return as the energy of light you have always been. If you could shine as bright for yourself and others here, right now as you do in heaven imagine what you could change for the better. Think about that.

I don't write about my life for you to believe it is the gospel truth. I write my truth so others might read it and discover validations of their own.

So I send this book out as I did the other with the energy that it goes where it will do the greatest good. I have no doubt that it will.

May your life be full of blessings as you Live, Love and Laugh your way home.

About The Author:

Deb Keckley was born and raised in Idaho. A place she still calls her home.

She has been a practicing medium for the last fifteen years, simply giving her time to help when she is guided to give a message.

You will always find a bit of the otherside in her stories, because she says, "Your life is your journey. You create it good or bad, but every now and then your loved ones in spirit are going to give you a little nudge to get you going in the right direction if you should hit a snag."

Deb's stories are born out of imagination. Scenarios of life that depict struggles against the negative with lessons that move us towards the positive life can be.

She says, " Just remember when your life gets tough. It never hurts to ask for a little divine intervention. You might be surprised to discover what can happen."

Made in the USA
Columbia, SC
30 September 2020